D1478378

Ball Pythons as Pets

Caring For Your Ball Python

Ball Python breeding, where to buy, types, care, temperament, cost, health, handling, husbandry, diet, and much more included!

By Lolly Brown

Copyrights and Trademarks

Disclaimer and Legal Notice

Foreword

Ball Pythons are named as such because of their habit of curling themselves up into tight balls, especially when they are frightened or under stress. They are the smallest of the African pythons, and they are also called Royal Pythons because African rulers are known to wear them as jewelry.

With their natural habitat being the African savannahs and grasslands, Ball Pythons have designs of browns and tans on their scales for camouflage, and their underbellies are typically ivory white. Some breeders in the pet industry, however, have managed to produce breeds with various morphs or genetic mutations that altered their patterns and colors, coming to include shades of yellow and gold, charcoal gray, and black.

Ball Pythons are considered to be one of the most well-mannered snake species and are known for their docile temperament. They have a long lifespan as well, making them ideal for long-term companionship. If you wish to have an exotic pet but are a relative beginner with reptilian ones, the curious and gentle Ball Python is perfect for you.

This book will provide you with relevant information regarding Ball Pythons, their nature and behaviors, and how to make sure that you will be giving them the utmost care.

Table of Contents

Introduction

When people think of pets, the first ones that come to mind are the classic choices – cats, dogs, birds, hamsters, and other usual domesticated animals. However, the number of people who want something more exotic and peculiar than the garden-variety furry creature is steadily increasing, and thus booms the demand for reptilian pets that include snakes.

Snakes, by nature, exude a certain kind of mystery for which some people have a preference. They are also relatively low key and quiet, and at the same time there is elegance in them that other animals cannot hope to match. Of course, there is also the additional panache that owning a pet snake gives to its owner; seeing as snakes are oftentimes portrayed as villains in any and all media types, showing how one can be tamed indeed leads to a certain advance in status or, at the very least, some bragging rights.

Snakes are seen as either friends or foes; they are enchanting or disturbing, delightful or terrifying. Obviously, snakes really do have a dangerous side for they are natural predators, and anyone who cannot account for this or is unwilling to embrace this fact should drop any lingering idea of keeping one as a pet. Snakes need dedication and determination in their care, and a prospective owner must be willing to exert effort to read up and completely comprehend what it means to take care of a snake and whatever duties that may entail.

If this is your first time taking a snake as a pet, then the Ball Python is perfect for you. Ball Pythons are the smallest of the African pythons, and they are considered to be one of the least aggressive snake species. They have a tendency to just curl up into a ball when provoked, hence the name, instead of displaying aggression, as other species are wont to do. Ball Pythons are well-mannered and well-tempered beings, and their docile temperament makes them rather popular as a pet choice. They also have a long lifespan, averaging at around 20 years, which means that those who choose to keep them must be prepared for a long-term commitment.

This book will be your guide and reference in caring for your pet snake. Be sure that you are prepared for the responsibilities that come with taking care of another living being, especially one as remarkably passive and amazingly gentle as the Ball Python.

Glossary of Snake Terms

1.2.3. (Numbers with full stops) – The numbers are used to denote the number of a species, arranged according to sex, thus: male.female.unknown sex. In this case, one male, two females, and three of unknown sex.

Acclimation – Adjusting to a new environment or new conditions over a period of time.

Active range – The area of activity which can include hunting, seeking refuge, and finding a mate.

Ambient temperature – The overall temperature of the environment.

Amelanistic – Amel for short; without melanin, or without any black or brown coloration.

Anal Plate – A modified ventral scale that covers and protects the vent; sometimes a single plate, sometimes a divided plate.

Anerythristic – Anery for short; without any red coloration.

Aquatic – Lives in water.

Arboreal – Lives in trees.

Betadine – An antiseptic that can be used to clean wounds in reptiles.

Bilateral – Where stripes, spots or markings are present on both sides of an animal.

Biotic – The living components of an environment.

Brille – A transparent scale above the eyes of snakes that allows them to see but also serves to protect the eyes at the same time. Also called Spectacle, and Ocular Scale.

Brumation – The equivalent of mammalian hibernation among reptiles.

Cannibalistic – Where an animal feeds on others of its own kind.

Caudocephalic Waves – The ripple-like contractions that move from the rear to the front of a snake's body.

CB – Captive Bred, or bred in captivity.

CH – Captive Hatched.

Cloaca – also Vent; a half-moon shaped opening for digestive waste disposal and sexual organs.

Cloacal Gaping – Indication of sexual receptivity of the female.

Cloacal Gland – A gland at the base of the tail which emits foul smelling liquid as a defense mechanism; also called Anal Gland.

Clutch – A batch of eggs.

Constriction – The act of wrapping or coiling around a prey to subdue and kill it prior to eating.

Crepuscular – Active at twilight, usually from dusk to dawn.

Crypsis – Camouflage or concealing.

Diurnal – Active by day

Drop – To lay eggs or to bear live young.

Ectothermic – Cold-blooded. An animal that cannot regulate its own body temperature, but sources body heat from the surroundings.

Endemic – Indigenous to a specific region or area.

Estivation – Also Aestivation; a period of dormancy that usually occurs during the hot or dry seasons in order to escape the heat or to remain hydrated.

Faunarium (Faun) – A plastic enclosure with an air holed lid, usually used for small animals such as hatchling snakes, lizards, and insects.

FK – Fresh Killed; a term usually used when feeding a rodent that is recently killed, and therefore still warm, to a pet snake.

Flexarium – A reptile enclosure that is mostly made from mesh screening, for species that require plenty of ventilation.

Fossorial – A burrowing species.

Fuzzy – For rodent prey, one that has just reached the stage of development where fur is starting to grow.

F/T – Frozen/thawed; used to refer to food items that are frozen but thawed before feeding to your pet.

Gestation – The period of development of an embryo within a female.

Gravid – The equivalent of pregnant in reptiles.

Glottis – A tube-like structure that projects from the lower jaw of a snake to facilitate ingestion of large food items.

Gut-loading – Feeding insects within 24 hours to a prey before they are fed to your pet, so that they pass on the nutritional benefits.

Hatchling – A newly hatched, or baby, reptile.

Hemipenes – Dual sex organs; common among male snakes.

Hemipenis – A single protrusion of a paired sexual organ; one half is used during copulation.

Herps/Herpetiles – A collective name for reptile and amphibian species.

Herpetoculturist – A person who keeps and breeds reptiles in captivity.

Herpetologist – A person who studies ectothermic animals, sometimes also used for those who keeps reptiles.

Herpetology – The study of reptiles and amphibians.

Hide Box – A furnishing within a reptile cage that gives the animal a secure place to hide.

Hots – Venomous.

Husbandry – The daily care of a pet reptile.

Hygrometer – Used to measure humidity.

Impaction – A blockage in the digestive tract due to the swallowing of an object that cannot be digested or broken down.

Incubate – Maintaining eggs in conditions favorable for development and hatching.

Interstitial – The skin between scales.

Intromission – Also mating; when the male's hemipenis is inserted into the cloaca of the female.

Juvenile – Not yet adult; not of breedable age.

LTC – Long Term Captive; or one that has been in captivity for more than six months.

MBD – Metabolic Bone Disease; occurs when reptiles lack sufficient calcium in their diet.

Morph – Color pattern

Musking – Secretion of a foul smelling liquid from its vent as a defense mechanism.

Oviparous – Egg-bearing.

Ovoviviparous – Eggs are retained inside the female's body until they hatch.

Pinkie – Newborn rodent.

Pip – The act of a hatchling snake to cut its way out of the egg using a special egg tooth.

PK – Pre-killed; a term used when live rodents are not fed to a snake.

Popping – The process by which the sex is determined among hatchlings.

Probing – The process by which the sex is determined among adults.

Regurgitation – Also Regurge; occurs when a snake regurgitates or brings out a half-digested meal.

R.I. – Respiratory Infection; common condition among reptiles kept in poor conditions.

Serpentine Locomotion – The manner in which snakes move.

Sloughing – Shedding.

Sub-adult – Juvenile.

Substrate – The material lining the bottom of a reptile enclosure.

Stat – Short for Thermostat

Tag – Slang for a bite or being bitten

Terrarium – A reptile enclosure.

Thermo-regulation – The process by which cold-blooded animals regulate their body temperature by moving from hot to cold surroundings.

Vent – Cloaca

Vivarium – Glass-fronted enclosure

Viviparous – Gives birth to live young.

WC – Wild Caught.

Weaner – A sub-adult rodent.

WF – Wild Farmed; refers to the collection of a pregnant female whose eggs or young were hatched or born in captivity.

Yearling – A year old.

Zoonosis – A disease that can be passed from animal to man.

Chapter One: Understanding Ball Pythons

The Python regius is the smallest of the African pythons. Because of its small size, passive temperament, and reasonable price, it has become one of the most popular pet snakes.

The Python regius is more commonly known as Ball Python because of the species' tendency to curl up into a ball when experiencing stress. Ball Pythons are also called the Royal Pythons, most notably in Europe, because they are used as jewelry by African rulers.

Ball Pythons typically have brown and tan colors for camouflage in the savannahs and grasslands, their natural habitat. Its underbelly is commonly ivory white or cream, and there are usually gold or light brown sides and dorsal blotches.

Ball Pythons are native to Africa, and their population is spread across the continent from Sudan and Uganda throughout Cameroon, Chad, and the Central African Republic and from Senegal, Mali, Sierra Leone, the Ivory Coast, and Nigeria. This snake species is also revered in Nigerian culture, particularly in its southeastern area, and are considered symbolic of the earth and its riches.

Ball Pythons are relatively easy to care for compared to other serpentine creatures, and their passive nature makes them an ideal pet even for children. They rarely bite, if at all, preferring to coil into a tight ball instead of facing aggression head-on.

They require regular handling to get them used to human touch, and constant touch makes them even tamer, making for wonderful and quite endearing reptilian pets.

Summary of Ball Python Facts

Kingdom: Animalia

Phylum: Chordata

Subphylum: Vertebrata

Class: Reptilia

Order: Squamata

Suborder: Serpentes

Family: Pythonidae

Genus: Python

Species: P. regius

Other Names: Boa regia, Enyrgrus regius, Cenchris regia, Python Bellii, Python regius, Hortulia regia

Common Names: Ball Python, Royal Python, King Python

Regions of Origin: Benin, Cameroon, Central African Republic, Côte d'Ivoire, Democratic Republic of the Congo, Gambia, Ghana, Guinea, Guinea-Bissau, Liberia, Mali, Niger, Nigeria, Senegal, Sierra Leone, South Sudan, Togo, and Uganda.

Primary Habitat: Grasslands, savannas, and sparsely wooded areas.

Description: Oval-shaped and narrow head, narrow neck, solid body, relatively short tail.

Length: 122 cm (4.0 ft) to 182 cm (6.0 ft)

Weight: Approximately 2 kg

Color: The Ball Python typically has brown and tan camouflaged designs, with the top of the head usually a dark brown, and its underside is ivory white or cream. There are a lot of naturally occurring color morphs within the species, including High Gold, Piedbald, Axanthic, Xanthic, Leucistic, Melanistic, and Albino. Juvenile Ball Pythons often have brighter and more yellow colorations compared to adult ones.

Conservation Status: Classified by the IUCN as "Least Concern" because of its large range and high, stable population. It is included in Appendix II of CITES (Convention on International Trade in Endangered Species of Wild Fauna and Flora), where the main threat is the species' capture for illegal trade.

Primary Behavioral Characteristics: Terricolous, nocturnal, sedentary, and solitary.

Health Conditions: Dermatitis, Respiratory Disease, Mouth Rot, Stomatitis, Ticks and Mites.

Lifespan: average 20 to 35 years

Origin and Distribution

The Ball Python is endemic to the grasslands and open forests of West and Central Africa. They are found in Benin, Cameroon, Central African Republic, Côte d'Ivoire, Democratic Republic of the Congo, Gambia, Ghana, Guinea, Guinea-Bissau, Liberia, Mali, Niger, Nigeria, Senegal, Sierra Leone, South Sudan, Togo, and Uganda, usually in plains, savannahs, and areas that provide them cover. They are also fond of areas cleared for farming, even often acting as pest control since they prey on mice and rodents.

Ball Pythons prefer areas close to a water source so that they can easily cool themselves during hot days. They also like empty mammal burrows and underground hiding spaces, where they spend most of their time, though they can also climb trees if they choose. They like their solitude and spend the day in tight crevices, and as nocturnal species, they are more active during nighttime, and are most active at dawn and at dusk.

Ball Pythons are not an endangered species. Though exploited for the pet trade, where approximately 30,000 to 50,000 Ball Pythons are annually imported from Africa to American markets, the decline in Ball Python population is not drastic enough to be considered a threat. Furthermore, the species has a large range and a wide distribution across the African continent. There are some areas, especially in Nigeria, where Ball Pythons are believed to be sacred and are thus protected accordingly.

According to the Convention on International Trade in Endangered Species of Wild Fauna and Flora or CITES, recent years have shown an increase in snake trade, with approximately 200,000 specimen involved. With the upsurge in demand, breeders put in efforts to make the snakes readily available for purchase, despite reptiles still being generally considered a rather unusual pet choice; after all, they are not easy to maintain, especially compared to the more typical household cat or dog.

Ball Pythons, though nowadays seen as the gentlest of the snakes, have been considered quite troublesome as recently as the 1990s, when they were taken as captives. This was largely due to the fact that those early-day captive snakes were adult snakes caught in the wild, thus not used to human presence. Today, though, being largely bred in captivity, the Ball Pythons' natural traits have adapted to be more suited to pet-keeping. Indeed, by the end of that decade, Ball Pythons had risen as high-profile snakes in herpetoculture.

The first albino Ball Python bred in captivity is the classic albino bred by Bob Clark. It has a pattern normal for Ball Pythons, except the patterns are white and orange gold, dark yellow, or yellow. It also has pink eyes and pink tongues. There is also the caramel albino Ball Python, which has yellow and medium purplish-gray patterns.

Since then, genetic basis and hereditary patterns have been discovered and experimented on, leading to developments in the breeding of Ball Pythons. Where at first there were only the regular Ball Pythons, albino Ball Pythons, and piebald Ball Pythons, today there are many various Ball Python morphs that are all gorgeous and breathtaking. These include Axanthic, Xanthic, Leucistic, Striped, Melanistic, and Banded.

Chapter Two: Things to Know Before Getting a Ball Python

This chapter will be focusing on some of the more practical concerns that you would need to consider before making the final decision of having a Ball Python as a pet. Information covered includes topics such as costs, licensing requirements, and the viability of keeping more than one Ball Python or the practicality of keeping them in the company of other snakes.

First of all, you should ask yourself exactly why you want to keep a Ball Python as a pet. Ball Pythons have an average lifespan of 20 years – suffice it to say that it is a considerable stretch of time, and if you are only considering getting a Ball Python as a status symbol, then you should rethink your choices. As much as Ball Pythons would make a wonderful addition to your household with their natural elegance and exquisiteness, their care would also demand much of your commitment. The responsibilities you would have to carry include feeding them, cleaning after them, seeing to their maintenance, and understanding their behavior.

Ball Pythons are gentle creatures, and their defense mechanism involves curling up into a tight ball of stress – rather surprising to some, really, in light of the usual mythos surrounding snakes. Ball Pythons also respond fairly well to human touch especially if it is constant, so you would have to make sure that you do not neglect them. They are known to be picky eaters and are sensitive to temperature, for which you will have to watch out. You will also have to check them constantly for ticks and mites, their primary parasites.

Simply put, Ball Pythons require a fair amount of guarantee that you will be there to take care of them and make sure they are okay. You cannot take care of a Ball Python halfway, and you have to be all in – starting with recognizing within yourself if you have what it takes to take care of this lovely creature.

Do You Need a License or a Permit?

There is no federal law governing private possession or ownership of exotic animals in the United States. You need to pay attention not on a national level but on a local level, with your local and state laws and ordinances, to see what is permitted and what is not. The regulations vary from locale to locale, as some outright ban or prohibit exotic or dangerous animals, while others simply call for permits that set down requirements such as microchipping, an established relationship with a veterinarian, and even insurance. Some may also ask you to present proof that you are acquiring the animal from a recognized breeder and that the snake was bred in captivity (as opposed to being captured from the wild).

Since the legalities may seem confusing, it is best if you consult with your local United States Fish and Wildlife Service Office to make sure that you are not inadvertently breaking any laws. It is also a good idea to check the rules about keeping pet snakes based on where you are - city, town, neighborhood, and even in the apartment building, if applicable. All these are reasonable precautions to take simply for the fact that should you ever be found to be keeping such a pet illegally, the discovery could result in consequences such as fines or, worse, the confiscation of your pet. You might not even be able to find a veterinarian willing to give your Ball Python medical care if you are found to be keeping it without the correct permits.

Permits may also be necessary for importing, exporting, or traveling with an exotic or a naturally dangerous animal. Additionally, since the Ball Python is included in Appendix II of the Convention on International Trade in Endangered Species of Wild Fauna and Flora or CITES, the international trade involving it is monitored and regulated.

You have to check under which classification the Ball Python falls – whether it is considered as an "exotic animal" or a "dangerous animal." Definitions may vary, including the process for getting a permit, which means that you would really have to do your research. You also need to be constantly updated on information regarding your local state laws at least once every six months. Regulations can change, and you don't want to find yourself suddenly in violation of a law which was amended after you thought you had abided by it a year ago.

If all this seems complicated and perhaps a tad overwhelming, keep in mind that you are bringing a potentially dangerous animal into a human community. As such, restrictions and limitations should be expected so that the safety of anyone involved will be ensured.

It must also be noted as a point of fact that the illegal trade in exotic animals has been an immensely profitable business for backyard breeders and illegal importers. In West Africa alone, many thousands are captured annually and exported, not all of them lawful. In Benin, for instance, illegal trade circuits involving the species are still active and have been linked to the food trade. Existing harvest practices affect the most susceptible biological stages – such as gravid females and neonates. Meanwhile, hunting techniques and methods – such as digging and destruction of burrows – affect the nesting habitat.

If you care about these animals at all, you shouldn't support activities which promote their unlawful capture from the wild or the breeding and transport of these animals in inappropriate and pitiless conditions.

How Many Ball Pythons Should You Keep?

Ball Pythons, being one of the most well-mannered python types, are an ideal choice for first-time snake-keepers. As a docile snake species, they adapt rather well with regular human contact. Their non-aggressive nature makes them suitable company for children as well. Since they are also the smallest of the African pythons, sometimes only exceeding four feet in length, they wouldn't be needing as much space as their bigger brethren. They are also generally shy creatures and would probably just spend their time hiding in a corner, especially when they are still not used to their owner's presence.

Just like when considering other pets, the decision of whether you can keep more than one Ball Python or not depends on your overall capacity to commit to all of them. Additionally, because of the good temperament Ball Pythons usually have, they are capable of peacefully sharing a burrow with others of its kind, should you actually end up getting more than one.

Of course, you must also keep in mind that keeping more than one Ball Python means an increase in responsibility and concerns – financially, timewise, and even mentally. Efforts of cleanup and cage maintenance will be doubled, or tripled, if you're feeling quite up for it. Before committing to such a huge undertaking, you should objectively assess your capacity to provide what your pets will require without fail. You will have to be completely ready and prepared; taking care of one Ball Python is already a lot, and more than that is quite daunting indeed. Be sure to make an informed and responsible decision on how many Ball Pythons you can responsibly and dutifully care for and keep.

Do Ball Pythons Get Along with Other Pets?

The Ball Python is a carnivorous natural predator, and when in the wild, they kill their prey by constricting it. Adult Ball Pythons are known to feed on adult mice, rats, or young chickens. Despite this, Ball Pythons are generally shy creatures, especially the ones bred in captivity, and they pose no real threat to your dog, cat, or child. If they feel threatened at all, they do not show aggression but rather draw back to their defense mechanism, which is curling into the tight ball for which they are named.

To be honest, perhaps it is the other animals that you should be wary of – sharp claws might hurt your Ball Python and not the other way around. Furthermore, since Ball Pythons do not make a lot of noises, you will also have to watch out that they haven't found themselves in places they shouldn't be when you let them out of their enclosure. They have a propensity for tight spaces, after all, and you wouldn't want to have a missing Ball Python only to later find it curled up in a hidden corner.

As stated before, Ball Pythons are docile and gentle, and they are the recommended snake to have if you have a child, though, of course, some supervision is still required just in case. Their willingness to be handled makes them the perfect pets, regardless of whether or not you already have other, furrier ones in your household.

How Much Does it Cost to Keep a Ball Python?

A Ball Python may cost anywhere from $50 to $3,000, depending on the type, quality, age, and breeder. Wild-caught Ball Pythons are cheaper than those bred in captivity, but it is not recommended that you get one from the wild as you will encounter more issues such as difficulty for the snake to settle in their new home and a host of potential health risks. Albino Ball Pythons are also more expensive than the regular ones, and those with rarer morphs even more so.

Of course, the money you would have to spend would not be limited to just the purchase price. You have to consider shipping costs and procurement of necessary permits, especially if you are ordering one from an international market. Shipping fees start at about $30 and will increase depending on the area of origin and delivery place. Also, you must be in possession of a proper enclosure before actually acquiring the snake – it is not recommended that you have the snake before having a proper place to keep it.

Alternatively, you may also consider adopting a rescued Ball Python. Usually, this type of Ball Pythons came from owners who perhaps lost interest in taking care of their pet or had some issues that made them not any more suitable to care for their pet. Getting a rescued Ball Python will cost you less, though you would still have to check with a veterinarian to ascertain that the snake is in robust condition, or maybe even to coax them back to health if needed. Ball Pythons can adapt quickly to new owners so long as their environment and required living conditions – such as appropriate enclosure, temperature, and substrate – are properly maintained.

You can also ask around your nearest animal rescue to see if they have any Ball Pythons. Check out the following site that offers the adoption of Ball Pythons and other reptiles in central Arkansas area:

Reptile Rescue Center

<http://www.reptilerescuecenter.org/reptiles-for-adoption/>

Aside from the purchase price, the greatest expense you will incur for your Ball Python is probably a well-provisioned enclosure. This includes heating, lighting, substrate, and proper furnishings. Other costs include veterinary checkups and electricity costs for heating and humidity.

Moreover, if your Ball Python cost you a large sum for purchase alone, say around $1,000, it is a good idea to have it insured. It is also wise to always have spare cash handy in case emergencies involving your snake that you might not have thought of beforehand happen. You should also take into account the costs of a permit or license, the fees of which are subject to change depending on your state or township laws and regulations.

Of course, you should not forget about food and how much feeding your snake will cost. Though not needing constant feeding especially when they are adults, Ball Pythons are known to be picky eaters, especially during winter months. Ball Pythons typically eat mice, but it is recommended that you convert them to eating rats as soon as possible. An adult Ball Python should be fed frozen-thawed food, since older rodents have developed teeth that can damage the snake upon ingestion.

Below is a broken-down summary of approximate annual cost you may incur in taking care of a Ball Python, specified in rounded figures:

Annual Costs for a Ball Python Snake	
Annual License or Permit Fees	$25-30
Veterinary Care	$100-125
Feeding	$50-200
Tank	$100
Lock-down top	$30
Heating bulb	$50-75
Electricity consumption	$300
Under Tank Heater	$25-30
Substrate	$15-25
Miscellaneous (water bowl, climbing branches, fake foliage, cleaning supplies, etc.)	$25-50
Total	**$720 to $965**

Keep in mind that these are just approximations. You may find cheaper alternatives in the market. Reputable breeders also allow for some negotiations in purchase price, especially when they see that you are serious about taking care of the snake.

You should also watch out for additional costs that will crop up over time, such as changing light bulbs, replacing the enclosure's foliage, and perhaps replacing the enclosure itself once your snake gets bigger. This is especially true since baby snakes get stressed in large enclosures, so you would have to make sure that the appropriate proportions are met.

What are the Pros and Cons of Ball Pythons?

If you're still uncertain whether a Ball Python is a good pet for you, you can consult the following lists of pros and cons that you might want to consider before making a final decision. The lists cover information relating to keeping an actual snake as a pet, with other factors that relate only keeping a Ball Python specifically.

Pros for the Ball Python

- Ball Pythons are naturally gorgeous creatures
- Ball Pythons have a specially docile and passive temperament
- Ball Pythons are not an endangered species and are thus more easily allowable by law to be kept as pets
- Ball Pythons, being the smallest of the African pythons and growing only five feet maximum – half a regular boa constrictor's length – do not require huge spaces
- Ball Pythons are generally low-key and shy, so if you're not up for a petting session, it's okay (though

regular exposure to humans does help in taming them more)

- Ball Pythons live a very long time, given proper care; one report stated a Ball Python living for up to 47 years
- Ball Pythons, unlike other animals, do not smell, so you wouldn't have to worry about stink or the need for an impromptu bath, unlike dogs

Cons for the Ball Python

- Ball Pythons are notoriously picky eaters, especially during winter months; you should watch out that they do not lose weight or starve
- Snakes, in general, and Ball Pythons, in particular, cannot be trained to do party tricks; if that's what you're looking for, you should perhaps just get a dog
- Ball Pythons are sensitive to temperature and humidity changes, so you would have to be extra careful to make sure that they are comfortable
- Finding a vet clinic well-equipped enough to treat your Ball Python should the need arise can be tricky, depending on the area where you live
- Finding a friend willing to feed your pet if you are not around is difficult, since most humans don't take kindly to feeding snakes lest their fears of being eaten themselves come true

- Speaking of feeding snakes – this is a task not recommended for the squeamish and the faint of heart; if you cannot bear to look at a rodent being devoured, then you should not get a snake as pet

- If you're looking for affectionate pets, then you should probably not be looking for a reptile at all

Chapter Three: Purchasing Your Ball Python

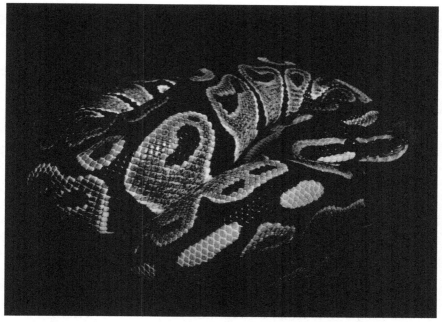

By this point, you are hopefully more informed about the Ball Python than before. If you have made your mind and decided that yes, the Ball Python is the pet you want, and that yes, you understand the responsibility of taking care of it, then the next step would be going about actually purchasing the snake.

You have to devote time and effort into doing research and read up materials to find a reputable breeder. You have to be willing to ask questions and make visits as well, and having a discussion with the breeder is a wise move. If you are not particular in choosing the breeder, and thus the pet, can result in you getting a Ball Python with health problems and erratic behavior, especially if it ended up being caught from the wild instead of actually being bred in captivity.

Having a discussion with a reputable breeder also ensures that your pet wouldn't be caught up in anything illegal. Besides, having someone who knows what they are doing can help you when the time comes, and you can ask for more hands-on advice that will enrich your understanding of the creature.

Some of the basic things you would have to consider when doing your research on which Ball Python to get would be sex, age, and morph. Do you want a male or female, a mature or a juvenile? Which color scheme would want – an albino, an axanthic, a xanthic?

When you have made your choice, you should then look for and prepare the enclosures – a smaller one if you want a hatchling or a juvenile Ball Python and a large one if you want a mature Ball Python. Be sure that the enclosure and everything that should be in it are properly set up and ready before bringing the Ball Python home.

You should also acquaint yourself with the local breeder from whom you can source the Ball Python's food. Of course, you should also find a clinic that is equipped with dealing with Ball Pythons and a veterinarian who is well-informed and experienced as well. A proper network within the community never hurt anybody, and would indeed help you in taking care of your Ball Python down the line.

Where Can You Buy Ball Pythons?

Finding a Ball Python for sale isn't really difficult, especially since they are one of the most popular snake breeds in the market. They are, in fact, quite easy to acquire and are relatively common compared to other snake species. You can find Ball Pythons for sale through:

- Looking for online vendors and breeders
- Going to a pet store
- Attending reptile expos

It is highly recommended that you purchase directly from the breeder, since this will provide you with a proficient source of information regarding the python's bloodline, lineage, and husbandry. Additionally, since most breeders who enter this field do so because of a genuine passion for the creatures they breed, you will also find them to be quite knowledgeable about the species that they breed.

However, you should also bear in mind that there are other factors that you need to consider in choosing where to make your purchase. While purchasing directly from a breeder does have its advantages, such advantages may not always be true for all breeders.

For instance, breeders can range from small, private breeders to mass producers that supply large quantities of pet animals to retailers and pet stores. Large-scale breeders sometimes may charge more because of the huge overhead they incur in their breeding processes, but sometimes small and private breeders may also charge quite a bit, especially if they are dealing with a particularly rare species. (A Ball Python with a ghost morph, for example, can cost you thousands of dollars.)

Consulting with breeders and their willingness to entertain questions you might have may reflect on the final fee you would have to pay. Breeders may be available to you and your queries at the right price, though, of course, there are those who are genuinely happy to help out a snake-keeper. Some pet stores also hire people who are quire informed about the creatures they are selling, so you can always try your luck in asking the personnel. Reptile expos, where reptile and snake enthusiasts often converge, are also a good place to look for people passionate about the animals and would be more than willing to answer questions about the creatures.

Meeting with people is a good way to gauge if they are actually decently informed or if they are just trying to make the sale – not that it is necessarily a bad thing, but sometimes important details are overlooked or left unsaid that may present a future problem. So it is recommended that you speak to them yourself and see if you find them trustworthy and reliable. Do they falter when answering your questions? Do they offer you helpful advice? Are they accommodating or hesitant? You should note how comfortable they are in providing the answers and how easily they give the information. Building a rapport is also ideal, since these people may be the ones to help you out should you encounter problems with your snake in the future.

How to Choose a Reputable Ball Python Breeder

Should you decide to cut out the middleman and head straight for the source, you should be sure that you know which source is actually worth going to. You should know how to choose a reputable breeder.

Breeders range from large-scale operations to small-scale, private setups. Some have legit websites filled with snake facts and official sources, and some have blogs that detail personal accounts of handling snakes and other reptiles – both of these often put up online advertisement, which is frankly the most popular form of advertisement nowadays. Some breeders, however, opt for a more formal and traditional route, attending reptile expos and showing off their breeds. Some, still, choose to work a bit behind the scenes and supply pet stores instead of putting up their own store. With such diversity, how can you choose what is good and what is not?

The first, and best, thing to look for when looking for reliable breeders is a good reputation – normally reflected on positive feedback and review. Join up online forums and discussions to see which ones are the big names in breeding high-quality Ball Pythons. Read up on articles with good sources, and check other comments if you can.

Breeders, just like other professionals, build their reputation through years of hard work and dedication to their craft. Where architects have lists of buildings under their belts, breeders have a list of satisfied customers. They may vouch for him, his breeding process, and his snakes as well. If a positive word from a veterinarian can be had, that will solidify his status even more.

Again, you should be certain of the snake you want to buy – age, sex, and type must be settled before looking for it. You should also be familiar enough with the requirement caring for the snake will entail, and you should be informed of behavioral quirks that may be found in the species. See that you are cognizant of the peculiarities usual in Ball Pythons, so that you won't be surprised when you encounter one for real.

Having a clear idea of what you want in a Ball Python will help limit your search parameters for breeders, and will help you focus on what you want to see. Concentrating on breeders specializing in Ball Pythons, furthermore, will save you precious time and energy. You will also be able to ask more relevant questions pertaining to the Ball Pythons in particular and not to snakes in general.

Ball Pythons are appropriate choice of pet for first-time snake-keepers, so you shouldn't encounter too much problems. Breeders will give you a wider leeway in asking obviously beginner questions, while reputable breeders will also make sure that you are up for the challenge of caring for the snake. Reputable breeders may offer you a 30-day health and customer satisfaction warranty, though perhaps this goes both ways – you will see if the snake is a good sort, and they will see if you are a good owner.

Last, but not the least, it is ideal that you purchase locally than source from the international market, or even just a distant area. Long distance keeps you from meeting the breeder face-to-face, and by extension, from seeing your intended purchase for yourself. Though not all bad, if you are certain that the breeder is legit, it still helps if you meet them in person.

Making your purchase from local breeders would allow you this opportunity, and you may be given the possible advantage of being allowed a visit or a tour of their facilities – and see for yourself that the setup is clean, organized, and ideal for the animals. In such a visit, you can build rapport and an inside connection that you would need when time for actual purchase comes, and it is always good to have someone knowledgeable about the species in your corner. During the first few weeks with your Ball Python, for instance, you might find yourself in need of professional advice, and having someone you can readily call will prove to be advantageous for you and your pet.

Tips for Selecting a Healthy Ball Python

After selecting a reputable breeder that you are comfortable with, it is time for you to decide on the Ball Python that you will be bringing home.

Regardless of what age, sex, or size python you are looking for, you are looking for a healthy animal with no illnesses or diseases, and as much as possible, no temperamental issues that would make things difficult for you when it comes to general snake husbandry such as feeding or cleaning their cage.

No matter what age, sex, or size python you are looking for, you should make sure that the animal is healthy. Signs of health in a Ball Python are a well-rounded body and clean and clear eyes and vent. There should be no signs of respiratory problems, such as wheezing when held, mouth opening a lot, nasal discharge, and mucus around or large bubbles in the mouth. They should also be free of parasites such as ticks and mites.

Though shy in general, the Ball Python must be somewhat curious and open to your touch, gripping you when being handled. See how the Ball Python feeds as well, if at all possible. This would give you a working idea of how the snake feeds, whether you are going to encounter feeding problems, picky as they are in nature, and whether they have been trained to readily feed.

Chapter Four: Caring for Your New Ball Python

One of the most important things to consider when you finally have your Ball Python is to set up a proper habitat for them. The conditions of this habitat should be likened from their natural one, ensuring that the Ball Python will flourish.

The natural habitat of Ball Pythons is in the wild life mainly in the savannahs, grasslands, and sparsely wooded forests. They are terricolous creatures, which mean that they live on the ground. Indeed, Ball Pythons have a tendency to seek out burrows and crevices and hide in dark spaces. More often than not, you will find them shying away, curling up into tight balls – a defense mechanism they use especially when stressed. They do know how to climb trees, though, and may do so when they fancy.

These are generally solitary creatures, like most snakes, and they are also nocturnal. They are most active on dusk and dawn. Ball Pythons are carnivorous, and they have mobile upper and lower jaws. Being non-aggressive, they sit and wait to ambush prey instead of going head on. In the wild, they either swallow the prey alive or immobilize it through constriction.

Housing a Ball Python should take into account lighting, temperature, humidity, and the presence of ample foliage it can hide on or climb.

The Basics of Reptile Thermoregulation

Thermoregulation is the act by which an animal controls or regulates his body temperature. For warm blooded animals such as mammals and birds, this is done through a combination of internal processes and external factors. For reptiles such as snakes, however, thermoregulation is exclusively an external matter.

Snakes and other reptiles are classified as ectotherms, which mean that they have no internal means of regulating body heat or metabolic function – as opposed to endotherms like mammals and birds that rely partly on caloric intake for energy. Snakes rely entirely on external sources for means of regulating their body temperature – either to stay warm or to keep from overheating. This is why the environment you prepare for your Ball Python is crucial.

There are three ways by which snakes and reptiles regulate their body temperature:

- Gaining heat via radiation, such as sunlight
- Gaining heat via conduction, such as when the ground temperature is higher than its body temperature
- Losing heat via convection, or when the air temperature is lower than its body temperature

You can observe thermoregulation activities among snakes and reptiles in the wild through various activities: they could bask in sunlight while lying on a rock, or they could seek shelter in the shade and away from direct sunlight. Essentially, they would have to move to where it is warmer or cooler, depending on what their body needs. In artificial conditions such as in an enclosure or terrarium, you will have to provide them with heat source that is variable enough within the enclosure so that they can seek a cooler spot should they need it. Among snake keepers, this is called a heat gradient. This is particularly important for Ball Pythons, known to be especially sensitive to temperature changes.

Ball Python Caging

A Ball Python requires an enclosure that should not exceed one and a half times its length and should not be less than two thirds its length.

Any decent enclosure hoping to keep its charge in should have a tight-fitting lid or door, preferably with a lock. The enclosure you choose should be one made especially to keep snakes, animals which are known to be quite skilled in the art of escape, and Ball pythons are especially clever and sneaky when it comes to breaking out. There are glass tanks with the combination of fixed screen and hinged glass top. A good starter tank for a hatchling is a 10-gallon tank (roughly 20"L x 10"W [50 cm x 25 cm]). A young adult requires a 20-gallon tank, and full adult may require a 30-gallon tank (roughly 36" x 12"W [91 cm x 35 cm]). Such sizes will help accommodate a Ball Python's normal behavior and exercise. The lid or other panels should be made of wire mesh to allow for good ventilation.

After you have bought your snake enclosure, the next step is to furnish it appropriately. Since Ball Pythons like to burrow, there must be a hide box in the cage, into which the snake can comfortably retreat, like a hollow log. This could be made from a wide terra cotta flowerpot. Enlarge the drain hole with a chisel and file it to remove any sharp edges, and place the pot in the cage, with the drain hole side up. The Ball Python will most likely spend most of the daylight hours in the hide box.

Shredded cypress or fir bark, paper towels, and newspapers provide a good substrate. Do not use pine or aspen as they can become lodged in your snake's mouth during feeding.

Additionally, your Ball Python should have a water bowl in the enclosure. Your snake will drink in it and soak itself in it, and sometimes, it may even defecate in it. Be sure to always check if it has been soiled and clean it up.

Heating Requirements

Temperatures in savannahs range from 68 to 86 degrees Fahrenheit. To be able to replicate this in a cage means providing supplemental heating sources – either baseline or hot spot, or both. An example of the former are under tank heater, and an example of the latter are basic light bulbs, ceramic heat emitters, or heat panels. All pythons, especially Ball Pythons, are very susceptible to thermal burns. Due to this reason, it is not recommended that you use a hot rock.

Enclosures must allow for a proper thermal gradient that the Ball Python can use, with a hotspot on one end of the enclosure and a cool spot on the other. You should provide a basking spot temperature of 88 to 96 degrees Fahrenheit and an ambient temperature of 78 to 80 degrees. The ambient temperature should not fall below 75 degrees.

Be careful when you select regular incandescent bulbs as one of your heat sources as this will also impact the lighting and day and night control cycles. You might want to pick out a ceramic heater to substitute occasionally for the bulbs, rotating them as needed, which would also keep down the risks of electrical overheating or malfunctions.

All artificial heating sources should be kept outside of the cage so as to protect the Ball Python from being burned. Invest in a good thermostat that would measure your temperature while also regulating the actual temperature inside the cage by automatically turning your heat source on and off as needed. You might also want to double check this manually, checking the cage with a regular thermometer to confirm the readings on your thermostat – which can certainly sometimes fail. Even with a thermostat, it is always a good idea to use a gauge.

Lighting Requirements

During a 24-hour period, snakes need at least 12 hours of light followed by 12 hours of darkness. A simple timer can help you regulate the lighting cycle.

Full-spectrum fluorescent lights will provide good lighting during the day. Unlike some reptiles, full spectrum lighting is not required for your Ball Python, though it still is recommended. The light can be slowly increased by 2 hours during summertime and decreased by 2 hours during wintertime.

Remember that you shouldn't use regular light bulbs that you can buy from your hardware store. There are specialized lights for reptiles that you can purchase from pet stores. These are intended to provide your pet with UV light that will supply your pet with the proper amount of UVA and UVB rays that your Ball Python will use in regulating their metabolism, to synthesize vitamins and minerals, and to metabolize calcium and help keep their bones strong. These types of lightning sources are intended to mimic natural sunlight as much as possible.

This photoperiod of 12 hours of light and 12 hours of darkness is important for snakes – particularly for nocturnal ones like the Ball Python. While you may be turning off the lights for your terrarium or snake cage for 12 hours, don't forget that room lighting can have a significant impact on the python. Once you have established your 12-12 hour cycle, try not to "shock" your pet by turning on the lights inside the room where they are kept during the 12 hours when it is supposed to be dark for them. This can lead to sleep deprivation, which can also lead to a number of other problems – whether it pertains to their health or temperament.

Be careful when choosing incandescent bulbs and the wattage they will consume. Higher wattage produces more heat, and this can significantly raise the temperatures within the enclosure.

Maintaining Humidity

A Ball Python's enclosure should be kept at 50 percent humidity. If the humidity is extremely low, a daily misting will provide the higher humidity that aids in proper shedding. Ball Pythons should not be kept in a damp environment since this can lead to skin infections and other problems in your pet.

Useful Tools and Devices

As long as the basic requirement for a proper habitat is met, taking care of your Ball Python will get relatively easier. The trickiest part would be keeping the temperature and humidity at their proper levels, but once that's done, you won't have to think too much about other details. Fortunately enough, there are a number of devices and gadgets that can help you monitor these pertinent environmental factors. Using these, you can make sure that your Ball Python's habitat is the closest it can be to its natural requirements. A mistake in any of these – light, heat, or humidity – can cause various problems in your pet such as illnesses or diseases, behavioral changes, and sometimes even death – such as if temperature rises too high and causes them to dry out.

Some of the tools or gadgets you should perhaps invest in and familiarize yourself with include:

- A simple light timer to automate the on/off cycles of your light sources
- A thermometer to help you measure the heat and temperature
- A thermostat to help you in regulating the temperature by turning heating sources on and off as needed

- A rheostat can act as a dimmer, reducing or increasing the amount of power that goes to a certain device such as a light or heat source
- A hygrometer to help you monitor the humidity levels

Chapter Five: Meeting Your Ball Python's Nutritional Needs

Ball Pythons are carnivores, and their diet in a natural environment consists mostly of small mammals such as rodents, mice, and small chickens. They either swallow their prey whole or, as constrictor snakes; wrap themselves around the prey to choke it.

Most snakes eat whenever they are happy or hungry. Unlike mammals, which need to constantly eat, snakes can go for prolonged periods without eating and still remain healthy.

This is particularly true of the Ball Python. The Ball Python, generally, are known to be particularly picky eaters. They often stop eating during winter months and during shedding periods, as well. Missing meals is not really a cause of concern for Ball Pythons, especially adult ones.

Ball Pythons go on fasting periods for a variety of reasons. Temperature, for instance, can affect their appetite. They can get antsy in too hot or too cold temperatures, thus they stop eating.

Ball Pythons are also reluctant when they encounter a food type they do not recognize – some, for example, prefer mice to rats, and when you change what you feed them, they will refuse to ingest it.

Ball Pythons also go off food whenever it is mating or breeding season. Breeding males stop go fasting from two to five months while breeding or simply if they can smell breed-able females.

Female snakes also refuse to eat in the later stages of their pregnancy, and after they ovulated. After laying their eggs, they can still continue their fast if they haven't been washed properly and the smell of their eggs still lingers.

Prey Items to Feed Ball Pythons

With a snake like the Ball Python, you will have to deal with the fact that you will have to purchase, store, and feed rodents of various sizes to your pet. This is not a field for the squeamish. You and the rest of your family will have to accept that there will need to be frozen little mice stored in a freezer in your home. Frozen packages of dead mice and rats of various sizes or ages can usually be bought from pet supply stores. For sanitary and health reasons, you should store these separately from your own food items.

It is always a good idea to sit down with your family and discuss this with them to make sure they are all on board. This would also minimize unwanted surprises should one of your family members one day rummage through the freezer for food items.

Prey items come in various sizes: pinkies, fuzzies, hoppers, weans, smalls, and adults. A Ball Python can eat prey larger than its heads, as the skin around its mouth is elastic in nature and allows it to engulf a large food item. However, just because your Ball Python can eat it doesn't mean you should feed it thus. It is recommended that you feed your Ball Python a frozen rodent that is no larger than the largest portion of its body. After being ingested, the swallowed prey item should just be large enough that your

Ball Python gets a slight bump - never a bulge - after having been consumed. It is always better to err on the side of caution and feed them smaller food items than to feed them rodent sizes that seem too large.

A general guide to feeding schedules is set out in the table below:

Stage	Frequency
Hatchlings	Once a week
Juveniles	Once of twice a week
Adults	Once every one or two weeks

Since Ball Pythons are nocturnal creatures, it is better if you feed them at night and with as little light as possible. While using a separate feeding enclosure may not always be necessary, some owners do prefer to feed their pythons in separate enclosures from their primary habitat to ensure greater ease in cleaning. If you are keeping more than one snake, a separate housing for feeding may prove to be necessary.

Feeding Fresh vs. Killed Prey

Many breeders choose to feed hatchlings on either live rat pups or mouse hoppers. If you are not amenable to this method, you can use a defrosted mouse hopper or fuzzy.

Keep in mind to never microwave frozen prey to thaw it. Exposure to extreme heat and pressure can make it explode - small food items tend to do this – and you may end up with prey guts all over the place. Instead, soak it in warm water until it is as close as possible to its live temperature. Achieving this temperature is especially important when you are feeding a hatchling; having it think its food is alive is more likely to elicit a strike or some sort of feeding response, since it is, foremost, a natural predator.

Whichever method you choose – whether live, pre-killed, or frozen – you should always be careful in feeding your Ball Python. It is terribly easy to stress them out during feeding time. This is why as a pet snake keeper; you may require hands-on assistance, patience, and persistence to be able to get through the feeding process. It does get easier over time, though, so you do not need to worry much.

Tongs are used to dangle the prey item near the Ball Python. Some might attack immediately and go after the food, but if they don't, you will have to entice the snake to feed. You can do this by:

- "walking" the prey as though it were still alive,
- rubbing it against your snake
- warming it until it has temperatures that are higher than room temperature make the prey item smell better by dipping it in a dish of warm chicken broth or piercing the prey's braincase with a pin to release more enticing odors.

Tips for Feeding Your Ball Python

- Pre-killed prey can be stored in a freezer for up to six months.
- Before feeding, pre-killed prey should be thawed completely and warmed to slightly above room temperature.
- Feeding frozen/thawed prey items reduces the chances of diseases and parasites in the snakes, and it also reduces the chances of injury.
- Never use your fingers to dangle food in front of your pet. Use tongs, tweezers, or a hemostat to handle prey items instead.

- This reduces your risks of snake bites as a ravenous snake can strike at anything that moves, and that includes your fingers.

- If your snake is not used to feeding on killed prey items, and you have decided not to feed them live prey, the habit of eating killed prey can easily be developed. Use the tips above that would make the prey more enticing for your pet. Remember to practice both patience and persistence as you train your python to feed on killed prey items. It can be challenging and even frustrating, but also rewarding and, in terms of long term care and feeding of your pet – will ultimately prove worthwhile

- On the other hand, don't overfeed your pet, either. Overfeeding will not only result in obesity, but in some animals, this can also cause prolapse

- Use slow, deliberate movements when you are feeding your snake. Snakes can react aggressively to sudden movements – either as a defense mechanism or because of its predatory instinct. Once you have successfully fed your python, and the snake has the foot clamped firmly in its strong jaws, don't make any sudden or jerky movements. Allow it sufficient quiet and undisturbed time to finish swallowing the entire meal.

- Fresh water should be available to your pet at all times. Snakes will use readily available water to either drink from, or to soak in, so the bowl has to be large enough to accommodate your pet, allowing it to fully submerge. This will help the snake when it comes time for them to shed. Clean and refill the water bowl at least twice a week.

Possible Feeding Problems

A healthy snake should have a healthy appetite, and will eat regularly. But what if they refuse to eat? As long as they are eating, you can be reasonably certain that they are getting sufficient nutrients from their food. A few other possible feeding problems include:

- Refusal of a meal several times in a row
- If your snake regurgitates its meal
- Obvious weight loss
- Signs of disease such as fluid or bubbles in the nostrils, sneezing, or open-mouthed breathing.

If you aren't sure about what you're doing, you can really injure the snake – whether in your handling of them or in how you feed them. Don't force feed your Ball Python just to get him to eat – especially if you do not have experience. Force feeding requires handling the snake while you force food down its throat using tongs or tweezers. It is best to take them to a veterinarian first so that you can identify the cause of your pet's feeding problems.

Chapter Six: Ball Python Husbandry

Snake keepers use the term "husbandry" to refer to the regular and daily care of a pet snake. Two of the most important facets of snake husbandry have already been discussed in the previous chapters: housing and feeding. In this chapter, we take a look at some of the other aspects types of husbandry care and maintenance that you will need to do to make sure that your Ball Python is kept clean, safe, and in good health.

Cleaning and Disinfecting the Snake Cage and Habitat

Aside from providing appropriate heating, lighting, humidity, and cage structures and décor, you will also want to clean your Ball Python's habitat enclosure regularly. This is particularly important as the prevailing humidity within the enclosure can be a perfect ground for the growth of bacteria. Most reptiles can be prone to skin and bacterial infection if left alone in unclean surroundings for long.

Regular cage maintenance and cleaning should be part of your routine. Not only will this keep the interior of the enclosure clean, odor-free, and healthy, but it will also keep you and your family safe and healthy. Regular cleaning prevents the possible transmission of diseases like Salmonella, which can be found in the fecal matter of reptiles, and which may be transmissible to humans.

Spot cleaning the interior of the cage should be done as often as possible – at least once a day, or once every other day. Spot cleaning your reptile's cage can include:

- The removal of fecal matter as soon as you notice them
- The removal of shed skin
- The removal of uneaten food
- Cleaning and refilling the water bowls at least twice a week

A more thorough cage cleaning should be done at least once a month, ideally more. During this process, you will need to relocate the snake so that you can clean and sterilize the entire cage components, including perches, decorations, substrate, etc. To be able to do this thoroughly, you will need to temporarily relocate your python to a different holding cage or cell. As usual, make sure that this cage is secure and clean, and is sufficiently ventilated.

- Remove all of the cage items, disposing directly of the substrate which you will be replacing completely. Set aside these cage items in a bowl or container. You will now proceed to clean the inside of the terrarium or cage, and then later on to disinfect and sterilize the cage items. Gather the following materials to help you in your cleaning tasks:
  - A spray bottle
  - Brushes, Q-tips, putty knives, or razor blades
  - Buckets
  - Terrarium cleaner that is safe for reptiles
  - Paper towels
  - Robber gloves
  - Sponges

- Learn to unplug everything! Make sure that all the electrical components of the cage – such as heating and lighting, are turned off or unplugged. Then armed with a spray bottle, a sponge, gloves, and just regular soap and water, begin to clean the interior of the snake cage as thoroughly as possible. Make use of instruments such as brushes, Q-tips, putty knives, or razor blades to really get at the hardened feces or waste that a regular paper towel won't be able to dislodge. Really get into it, using herp-safe terrarium cleaners for the really troublesome spots and corners. Rinse the inside of the cage thoroughly.

- The only way to be sure is to kill any thriving bacteria through high heat and boiling temperatures as you thoroughly sterilize each cage item. Clean and disinfect the cage items by boiling them in water for some 30 minutes. Try to avoid using regular household chemical cleaners which may prove toxic or harmful to your pet. Besides, even using these types of cleansers cannot really guarantee the thorough elimination of bacteria.

- Use a disinfectant to give another through cleaning to all the cage items, including the interior of the snake cage. Then use hot water to rinse of all chemical residues. Allow it all to air-dry, making sure that the cage interior and all the various cage items and implements are thoroughly dried.

- After doing the steps above, reinstall all the cage items and decorations, this time putting on a new layer of fresh substrate. You might also want to give your Ball Python a bath before allowing it to return to its newly cleaned and dry terrarium.

Wash and disinfect all your cleaning tools and equipment with the same thoroughness that you practiced when you were cleaning the cage interior and the cage items. And finally, wash your hands thoroughly – using hot, soapy water. Don't forget to finish off with a disinfectant, too.

Tips for Bathing a Ball Python

Bathing a pet snake is a simple and straightforward process – but with loads of benefits for your pet. An occasional bath for your Ball Python can therefore go a long way to having a happy and healthy snake. Bathing can help relieve constipation in your snake, and it can also kill mites and promotes shedding.

Use warm spring or filtered water. Don't use tap or chlorinated water as the chemicals in the water can actually irritate their skin. A good range between 100 and 105 degrees Fahrenheit is a good level for a snake bath. And because they are sensitive to temperature changes, you'll want to provide them with a reasonably warm bath.

You can help your snake get into the bath, but more often than not, they will quickly bathe themselves. You don't want your Ball Python getting away from you during bathing time; you might want to place a sufficiently roomy bowl of the warm bath water in an enclosure.

Just let your Ball Python swim freely around in the water. If it shows signs of agitation, take it out immediately. Otherwise, let it soak around for 10 to 15 minutes. When it is done, pick it up, gently use a towel to dry it off, and then return it to his now clean, sterilized, disinfected, and thoroughly dried habitat.

Some recommend placing your snake in a holding cage immediately after a bath as some snakes can defecate immediately after a bath, and you don't want him doing this too soon within the newly cleaned cage. Give your python sufficient time in the holding cage to do his business before moving him back to his home.

Chapter Seven: Ball Python Handling and Temperament

Ball Pythons, as established in earlier chapters, are docile, gentle, well-mannered creatures. They very rarely bite, only under extreme duress.

They have a passive nature. Instead of facing aggression head on, they merely curl their long bodies into tight balls – the very same instinct that earned them their moniker. They are also a lot more tolerant of human handling and care. This makes Ball Python an ideal pet choice for beginners in pet-keeping and for children.

Ball Python Temperament

The more they experience human touch, tamer a Ball Python will get. They are solitary and shy. They tend to spend their time hiding in a burrow or some tight, dark space, which is why a hollow log or some sort of hiding box should be placed in their enclosure. However, they do tolerate being kept in the same enclosure as other snakes, provided that they are the same species.

Ball Pythons get stressed when they experience change in their environment, but if the conditions of their natural habitat can be appropriately replicated, they can adapt easily.

Tips for Handling Your Ball Python

Read below for some tips and guidelines to keep in mind as you handle your Ball Python pet. Pay attention to the snake's responses - often enough, your pet's reaction will vary – based on the stress they may feel or how you approach them. Remember to always to keep calm and to make your actions slow and deliberate. Other influencing factors could be individual and varying temperaments between individual snakes – not all will react the same way, and this is mostly due to their individual experiences of being handled.

They can be very tame as time goes on and they get more used to touching and handling. Though snakes are generally not tactile creatures in general, Ball Pythons in particular are relatively tolerant of human touch.

Juvenile Baby Pythons, though, are a bit more secretive and are easy to stress. As they grow, their timidity lessens and they begin to crawl around and explore their habitat. They spend most of their time all balled up or hiding in their shelters. They even sometimes initiate contact by trying to climb their owner's arms. Do be careful about leaving them unattended, though, because Ball Pythons are notorious escape artists.

- Never pick your Ball Python up by the head. Almost all snakes tend to thoroughly dislike being petted on their head, as it makes them feel like you are a predator exerting dominance. This will stress them out and may cause them to bite you – a rare occurrence in their species, but may be a result of instinct.
- Just as well, never pick up your snake by the tail alone either. Doing so may cause it to thrash around in your grip and may end up injuring itself.

- Support and lift your Ball Python from the mid-body area. It will relax better in your grip.
- Be extra careful in handling your juvenile Ball Python, as it is also extra shy and extra nervous. Be prepared for the possibilities that it may crawl away from you – juveniles tend to pick the "flight" instinct in "fight or flight," and this is especially true of as passive a species as a Ball Python.
- Let the Ball Python become accustomed to your handling. Be gentle and slow in your touch.
- Be sensitive and gauge how they react to your touch. Pay attention to how your Ball Python responds to your movements. After all, it isn't a dog or a cat that can whine, purr, or bark to let its feelings be known.

Behavioral Characteristics of the Ball Python

This section contains a general guideline on the behavioral characteristics of the Ball Python – each of which should be useful during the handling and husbandry of these snakes.

Although Ball Pythons will have unique and individual character traits that the keeper will become familiar with after years of familiarity, there are common behaviors among all Ball Pythons that can be used as guide in reading the python's activities and conduct.

- Ball Pythons do not attack humans, and they ball up their bodies instead of fighting when provoked. Females, however, do show some protectiveness over their eggs and thus should be treated with more care.

- Ball Pythons, like most pythons, are constrictors – using their sharp, backward-curving teeth, they will grasp the prey to restrain it, and then wrap it around with coils. They do not usually crush their prey to death, as opposed to contrary beliefs – they simple asphyxiate their prey so that they may eat it easily.

- This is primarily a terricolous species, which means that they spend most of their time low on the ground. They are also nocturnal, doing most of their activities at night, and they are usually most active on dusk and dawn.

- The juveniles of this species like smaller places. They get extremely agitated and stressed if their enclosure is too big for them. They sometimes stop eating because they are daunted by the large space. They are shyer as well and would have to be gently coaxed to be properly handled. Small enclosures make them feel secure.

- These are ambush predators. They avoid detection, seek cover, and wait for their prey. Their hiding skills involve camouflage – which works very well in their natural savannah and grassland habitats – and, of course, curling up into a ball.

- Pythons have infrared-sensitive receptors in deep grooves in their snout, which allows them to "see" the radiated heat of warm-blooded prey. They use their forked tongues to both "smell" and taste – thus allowing them to track their prey – the tongues collect airborne particles which are passed on to the Jacobson's organ in the mouth for examination. They can also perceive movement through their undersides, which are sensitive to vibrations in the ground.

- Snakes have specialized belly scales which can grip surfaces and which they use to travel or climb. Snake scales are extensions of their epidermis – so shedding removes the complete outer layer as a single unit, rather than separately. This is called shedding, molting, or sloughing, and is useful in replacing old and worn skin while also getting rid of external parasites such as mites and ticks.

- Prior to shedding, the snake stops eating and retreats or hides in a safe place. The inner surface of the skin liquefies at this point, which separates the old skin from the new skin. When the snake is ready – typically after a few days – the eyes clear again and the snake crawls out of its old skin. The new skin is typically larger and brighter than the old one.

Their skin becomes dull and dry looking, and their eyes turn cloudy or blue-colored. Akin to a sock being turned inside out, the old skin breaks near the mouth, and through wriggling and rubbing against rough surfaces, the snake comes out of its old skin – which is peeled back over the body in one piece, from head to tail.

- While adult snakes may shed its skin only once or twice a year, younger or juvenile and growing snakes can shed up to four times a year.

Chapter Eight: Breeding Your Ball Python

Most of the Ball Pythons being kept as pets nowadays were bred in captivity. It has been easier to breed them since the 1990s, and the progress in breeding efforts has produced many beautiful morphs and genetic mutations.

Breeding season for Ball Pythons generally fall on the rainy months. They have long reproductive periods, lasting from about 27 months to 30 years.

Sexing

A successful breeding program begins with a healthy breeding pair. Females usually reach sexual maturity after 31 months, while the sexual maturity of males occurs after 18 years.

The process by which you can identify whether a snake is a male or a female is called sexing.

Sexing can be done in either one of two ways: by cloacal popping or cloacal probing. Please take note that you should never sex hatchlings. They are very sensitive and delicate at this stage, and attempting to sex them can injure them severely.

Cloacal popping is done by applying pressure with the thumb just below the vent. This will cause the hemipenes of a male to evert, one on each side of the cloacal opening. Females, on the other hand, may evert her cloaca and erect her scent gland papillae.

Cloacal probing is the more commonly employed means of sexing. It is done by gently inserting a lubricated probe – a slender stainless steel – into the side of the vent, and then sliding them into the pockets that are found on either side of the tail. For males, the probe will slide to a depth of approximately 10 scales, while for a female; it will go for only 3 or 4 scales. Sometimes the probe will only go somewhere between these two ranges, and these are often classified as unsexed snakes. Probing isn't always definitive or certain, and other factors may influence the result such as the pressure you exert on the probe, or something blocking the pockets so you could not insert the probe deep enough. It is essential that you don't try to attempt to probe your snake if you do not have sufficient experience with sexing. A mistake here can injure and damage your snake, and there is always the chance that the results of your probe can be wrong.

More often than not, a determination of a snake's sex can be established from their behavior. Males are generally more active than females. They also tend to refuse food during breeding time. But perhaps the best sign that your snake is a male is when he everts his hemipenes when he is defecating. When he sheds his skin, the hemipenes can be identified as two dried bits of skin at the vent – but which should not be confused with a small bump that can also show in the shed skin of females. Their tail shape can also differ, with the male's being more parallel and bulbous, as opposed to the female's tail which is more tapered in shape.

For a breeding pair, females should ideally be bigger and weightier than males. This is to allow them to have sufficient body weight that can undergo the stress of egg production. Females are usually paired only after they have reached 1,200 to 1,500 grams, which they can reach around the age of 3 or 4 years. Males, on the other hand, can be a lot younger and lighter; some use males that have reached 50 to 700 grams. The selected breeding pair must both be in good health, with good body weight and muscle tone.

Thermal Cycling and Cooling

Ball Pythons are sensitive to temperature and changes in their environment, and they usually start their breeding season based on those. In captivity, the same results can be stimulated by dropping the cage temperatures gradually over a period of time.

To be at par with the seasonal calendar, shut off heating and lights during nights around October. Let the temperature drop to as cool as 70 to 75 degree Fahrenheit, and let it last for 12 to 14 hours. Return the heat and lighting to normal during daytime, raising the temperature to about 85 to 88 degrees Fahrenheit. You can use timers to make this more convenient for you.

The point of changing up the temperature is to mimic what happens outdoors, with the drops in temperature starting around August until January. Note that you can dictate the terms of your breeding season by using an air-conditioning unit.

There are no hard and fast rules as to how long you should promote thermal cycling. Some breeders do this for around 3 or 4 weeks before finally placing the male with the female python.

Introduction and Mating

You will introduce the male to the female's cage once a week for two days to copulate. This process will be repeated for up to four months. The days between the two-day copulation periods will serve as the pythons' rest days. Breeders usually assign different females with which the make will copulate, with the ratio being three to five females to one male.

Ovulation and Pre-Lay Shed

During the weeks prior to ovulation, hard masses – called follicles – will start to be felt in the belly of female Ball Python. Note that these follicles are not eggs; rather, it is an egg cell surrounded by one or more layers of follicle cells. The follicle represents the genetic material the female parent will contribute to the offspring. The male's sperm will pass his half of genetic material to the offspring.

Ball Pythons really aren't gravid, or pregnant, prior to ovulation. At this point, the follicles still have not been fertilized by the sperm, so they cannot be considered eggs.

When ovulation does occur, the female will swell at about the last third of her body. This can last from 12 to 24 hours. It is easy to notice the swelling – it will look like a bulge from ingesting a particularly hearty meal.

This swelling resulted from the female's efforts to make the follicles pass into the oviducts, where they are fertilized in the oviducts by the sperm.

The sperm has traveled to this position in the female's body in the weeks or days after mating. Proteins and calcium are laid down in the oviduct. These nutrients will help to generate the shell. It is only by this point that the female can be considered gravid – she is carrying actual eggs. Eggs, whether they are fertile or slugs, cannot be reabsorbed, unlike the follicles.

There will be a pre-lay shed around 15 days after the ovulation period.

Laying Eggs

The gestation period for a gravid female Ball Python is approximately 43 days after ovulation, or around 28 days after the pre-lay shed. .

A nesting box should be provided for her in the cage – and this can be constructed of either wood or plastic, with a lid and an entrance hole large enough to accommodate the passage of two coils of her body at the same time. Some can use an improvised box, lidded plastic buckets, ice cream containers, or even overturned flower pots. A good size for the nesting box would be around 8 inches by 8 inches wide by 12 inches high. Lining should be provided at the bottom of the nesting box to prevent the eggs from sticking to the box itself. Some make good use of dry sphagnum moss, newspaper, coconut fiber, or vermiculite.

Be careful where you place the box in the cage – make sure that it is not directly connected or near a light and heat source or you risk overheating the eggs.

Sometimes, the female will refuse to use the nesting box you have provided for her. Some might lay the eggs directly while they are on the perch – so you need to provide a thick enough lining at the bottom of the cage to help cushion the eggs as they fall. Others might even choose to lay their eggs in the water bowl. To prevent the eggs from drowning, you might want to reduce the water content in the bowl to at least a centimeter or so when the time is nearing for the female to lay her eggs. There are even breeders who remove the water bowls and perches from within the cage altogether in preparation for the arrival of the eggs.

Brooding or Incubation

The average clutch size of a Ball Python is around 1 to 11 eggs. In the wild, the female broods over the eggs for a period of about 50 days more or less, during which she will refuse to eat until the eggs are hatched. For this reason, many breeders prefer artificial incubation to allow the female a faster recovery. Females typically refuse eating from the period of ovulation until hatching, and coupled with the physical demand of having produced and laid the eggs, the female's physical condition is at risk of deteriorating quite rapidly. A significant amount of weight loss is to be expected – which makes her recovery that much harder.

Opting for maternal incubation also makes it more difficult for you to check on the eggs. A single bad egg can cause the entire clutch to deteriorate, since the eggs typically adhere to each other. Thus some form of monitoring or examination of the eggs is important – something that would be difficult to do in cases of maternal incubation.

For all these reasons, artificial incubation is often considered the more feasible option. Fortunately, there are high-quality incubators readily available in the market for reasonable prices. Other breeders opt to build their own.

You need to remove the female from the eggs around which she would have coiled. Simply lift her coils until she is removed from the eggs. Many times this can be done without any fuss, but if you are dealing with a more aggressive female, you might need more than one person to help accomplish this – one to hold the female's head, and the other to lift her coils.

The eggs will often be stuck together in a clump. Separate them carefully to place them in individual trays to prevent bad or rotting eggs from contaminating the rest. Be careful as you do this so you do not tear the eggs, though a small tear is not necessarily fatal, and the egg can still go to full term to hatch.

Traditionally, incubation media of sphagnum moss, vermiculite and perlite were used with great success. More recently, however, most breeders have shifted to a no-substrate method of incubation where the eggs are suspended on a rack above a reservoir of water. This allows the incubation container to maintain steady levels of humidity without the egg coming into contact with moist or wet substrate media. This container is largely sealed, with only very small holes for ventilation. Occasionally, you should open the container to promote air exchange – at least once a week at first, then at least daily within the final week near hatching. Make sure that no condensation forms on the lid of the container which can cause moisture to drip down onto the eggs as this can cause the eggs to spoil. As much as possible, the eggs should not come into contact with or be exposed to wet or moist surfaces.

The incubation container should be maintained at temperatures of approximately 80 to 84 degrees. Humidity levels should also be maintained at above 90 percent throughout the incubation period, mayhap even at 100 percent. The incubation period lasts for around 60 days, after which the eggs are ready to hatch.

Hatching

Towards the time near hatching, replace the water at the bottom of the container with damp paper towels to prevent the drowning of any hatchlings that may emerge. You may also wish to provide a perch or two to provide them a place to rest after they have emerged from the egg.

Baby ball pythons use egg tooth to slit through the eggs, working their way out. Don't try to pull the hatchling out, or to help them out of the egg if this happens – they may still be absorbing some of the yolk from inside the egg. But if the egg begins to degrade and the neonate still refuses to leave, some gentle prodding will encourage it to finally move and exit from the egg.

At hatching, a neonate Ball Python measures approximately 20 to 30 cm in length and weighs in at an average of 65 to 108 grams. Their color will depend on the morph or genetic mutation the breeding has produced. Each of them should be set up in individual plastic tubs where they should be kept well-hydrated until they shed. Provide them with a simple perch, a water bowl, and a heat source.

Feeding should be initiated by tease-feeding the neonates with pre-killed or frozen/thawed pinkies that are no larger than the snake's diameter at mid-body. Some might initially be shy or retiring, and patience is required to get them to feed successfully. If an adult Ball Python is a picky eater, a hatchling is even more so.

Chapter Nine: Keeping Your Ball Python Healthy

This chapter will discuss the usual health problems a Ball Python contracts and suffers through, as well as the symptoms and the possible cures for it to get better.

Taking care of your Ball Python is a rather clear-cut matter. Provide it a well-designed cage with the proper equipment. Make sure its enclosure has achieved and is maintaining the correct specifications to create an environment where your Ball Python can live and thrive. Keep it clean. Keep it warm. Do not let your Ball Python starve, but do not force it to eat when it is not necessary, either. If you can do there, constantly, then chances are high that you and your Ball Python will spend together a long, long time.

However, as with most cases when dealing with pets, it is inevitable that at some point, your Ball Python may fall sick.

Most of the time, a Ball Python's health problems are due to their habitat falling short of the environmental specifications required of it, as in temperature, humidity, and cleanliness. This is why keeping your Ball Python's habitat enclosure is a very important thing.

You should also remember way before actually acquiring the Ball Python and taking it home, to have a good, trusted, and reputable veterinarian who is experienced and skilled in dealing with and treating reptiles and snakes. Keep in mind that not all veterinarians have worked on reptiles and snakes, since it is obviously not that common as a pet choice. A limited practical knowledge on the animals may do more harm than good.

Some of the various health conditions to which Ball Pythons are prone to include:

- Respiratory disease
- Vesicular dermatitis
- Inclusion body diseases

- Infectious stomatitis
- Ticks and mites

Respiratory disease

Respiratory disease is typically caused by bacteria, though some other causes are parasites, viruses, and fungi. In Ball Pythons, respiratory disease is usually observed with mouth rot.

Symptoms include excess mucus in their oral cavities, excessive nasal discharges, and loss of appetite. They may wheeze, may make gurgling sounds, or may have open-mouth breathing as well.

The veterinarian may take X-rays, blood tests, and cultures to determine the root cause of the disease. Treatment usually includes antibiotics, which may be administered orally, through injection, or by nose drops. Ball Pythons suffering from respiratory disease require intensive care, which may include fluid therapy and force feeding.

Dermatitis

Dermatitis in Ball Pythons is usually caused by an unclean habitat or damp surroundings, and it is typically characterized by blisters and rapid shedding.

Usually, the initial vesicles are filled with fluid and do not have any bacteria. However, in time, if the conditions are not corrected, any bacterial organisms found in or on the snake or its environment may infect the vesicles.

Sooner or later, if the infection is left untreated, the bacteria can spread through the bloodstream, thereby causing septicemia. In severe cases, death can occur in a matter of days.

If you think your Ball Python has this disease, then you should immediately place it in a dry environment and fix the humidity in its enclosure. Clean the habitat as well.

Go to the veterinarian before it gets worse. To determine which antibiotic treatment is best for the Ball Python, the veterinarian will have to perform diagnosis which may include a biopsy or cytology and a bacterial culture and sensitivity.

The Ball Python's chances for complete healing are higher if it still feeds and is still active.

Inclusion Body Diseases

Inclusion body disease (IBD) is a very serious viral disease. It may attack the Ball Python's respiratory or digestive track, but generally it goes for the snake's nervous system. Ball Pythons with IBD would not be able to lie on their backs and may even be paralyzed.

Ball Pythons, and other snakes, that are diagnosed with IBD are euthanized because there is no existing cure as of yet.

Infectious stomatitis

Stomatitis is also called mouth rot. It is an infection of the snake's oral cavity. There is usually an excessive amount of mucus, possibly with blood in it, in the mouth and at the inside edge of the lips. There is also pus, a white cheesy substance, in the mouth.

In severe cases, loss of teeth may be observed, as well as swollen mouth, open-mouth breathing, and loss of appetite.

Immediately consult the veterinarian when you think your Ball Python has contracted stomatitis – it can be fatal if left untreated. To cure stomatitis, injectable antibiotics would have to be administered to the Ball Python. Its mouth would also have to be thoroughly cleaned with antibiotic solutions.

Ticks and mites

Both internal and external parasites are common in snakes. Internal parasites include various worms, while external parasites include tick and mites. There is often no visible signs that your snake is infected with parasites, and it usually veterinary check-ups that reveal it so.

However, symptoms that your Ball Python may be suffering from parasites are breathing problems, diarrhea, and regurgitation, irritation on the scales, skin infections, weight loss, and swelling of internal organs.

Consult with the veterinarian. There are available medications to deworm the snake, which can be either ingested or injected.

Rectal Prolapse

Rectal Prolapse takes place when the bowel protrudes outside of the cloaca during defecation, whereby the snake subsequently is unable to retract it. Some point to inappropriate diet as the cause, though other contributing factors may also be obesity, stress, and lack of muscle tone. A lack of exercise and dehydration may also lead to rectal prolapse. It can be frightening when this happens, but usually looks much worse than it actually is.

Keep your snake well hydrated through their food, available fresh water, and humid conditions within the tank. This is also why it is important to have a good, sizeable enclosure for your Ball Python, with various perches to choose from. This encourages exercise and movement that can prevent this condition from developing in the first place.

There are some keepers who actually take their snakes out for a "walk" out on the lawn to introduce movement and exercise.

Bring your snake to a vet for proper treatment of rectal prolapsed. Sometimes a form of adhesive material that can later be easily pulled off, such as band aid, is used around the cloaca to prevent a reoccurrence of the prolapsed. This consists of moistening the swollen tissue and reinserting it back into place. This should be followed by withholding food for about two weeks, followed by controlled feeding of small prey until bowel movement normalizes.

Tail-hanging

When fecal matter accumulates, sometimes becoming very dry, it is no longer comfortable for the snake to wrap it around its perch, and is often simply left to hang suspended from its perch. This is similar to constipation among snakes, and is often related to or eventually causes rectal prolapse.

The effort to expel the accumulated feces is certainly greater, and the difficulty of doing so may lead to the rectal prolapsed where part of the bowel extrudes when they defecate, with the snake unable to retract it. Treatment thus proceeds as for rectal prolapsed in the section above.

Some form of exercise would help build your snake's muscle tone, as well as promote healthier digestive processes. As with most of the other conditions that can afflict snakes, this can possibly be prevented by integrating regular schedules and lifestyle routines that promote movement, exercise, and hydration in your pet snake.

Septicemia

Septicemia, also called toxemia, is a disease where microbes invade the bloodstream and other organs. When a snake contracts septicemia, it becomes critically ill and may even be near-death. Symptoms include lethargy, lack of appetite, red discoloration on the scale of the snake's belly, and open-mouth breathing.

Septicemia requires prompt treatment. If your Ball Python exhibits symptoms, bring it immediately to the veterinarian. Antibiotics and fluid therapy must be administered, and sometimes force-feeding is even necessary.

Ball Python Care Sheet

The most relevant information regarding the Ball Python and its care are offered in this chapter, making a quick search easier for you should you wish for a specific pertinent fact.

This section may also serve as a review or short refresher guide for you to remember the most important information to keep in mind to ensure that you and your serpent friend will share a long and happy life.

Basic Ball Python Information

Kingdom: Animalia

Phylum: Chordata

Subphylum: Vertebrata

Class: Reptilia

Order: Squamata

Suborder: Serpentes

Family: Pythonidae

Genus: Python

Species: P. regius

Other Names: Boa regia, Enyrgrus regius, Cenchris regia, Python Bellii, Python regius, Hortulia regia

Common Names: Ball Python, Royal Python, King Python

Regions of Origin: Benin, Cameroon, Central African Republic, Côte d'Ivoire, Democratic Republic of the Congo, Gambia, Ghana, Guinea, Guinea-Bissau, Liberia, Mali, Niger, Nigeria, Senegal, Sierra Leone, South Sudan, Togo, and Uganda.

Primary Habitat: Grasslands, savannas, and sparsely wooded areas.

Description: Oval-shaped and narrow head, narrow neck, solid body, relatively short tail.

Length: 122 cm (4.0 ft) to 182 cm (6.0 ft)

Weight: Approximately 2 kg

Color: The Ball Python typically has brown and tan camouflaged designs, with the top of the head usually a dark brown, and its underside is ivory white or cream. There are a lot of naturally occurring color morphs within the species, including High Gold, Piedbald, Axanthic, Xanthic, Leucistic, Melanistic, and Albino. Juvenile Ball Pythons often have brighter and more yellow colorations compared to adult ones.

Conservation Status: Classified by the IUCN as "Least Concern" because of its large range and high, stable population. It is included in Appendix II of CITES (Convention on International Trade in Endangered Species of Wild Fauna and Flora), where the main threat is the species' capture for illegal trade.

Primary Behavioral Characteristics: Terricolous, nocturnal, sedentary, and solitary.

Health Conditions: Dermatitis, Respiratory Disease, Mouth Rot, Stomatitis, Ticks and Mites.

Lifespan: average 20 to 35 years

Habitat Requirements

Recommended Equipment: Terrarium or snake cage/enclosure, water bowl, substrate, plants, driftwood, moss, and rocks, heat and light sources, thermometer, thermostat, light timer

Recommended Day/Light Cycle: 12-12 hours

Recommended Temperature: 80-85 degrees Fahrenheit

Recommended Humidity Levels: 50 percent

Cleaning Frequency: Daily cage cleaning with weekly maintenance, and everything put into the cage should be washed and disinfected weekly as well.

Nutritional Needs

Primary Diet: Mice and rats

Feeding Frequency (Hatchlings): once a week

Feeding Frequency (Juvenile): once or twice a week

Feeding Frequency (Adult): once every 1-2 weeks

Water: Fresh water in a bowl should be always available.

Breeding Information

Age of Sexual Maturity (Females): 27 to 31 months

Age of Sexual Maturity (Males): 16 to 18 months

Thermal Cycling: approximately 68 degrees Fahrenheit at nighttime

Copulation: 2 to 3 days

Gestation Period: 44 to 54 days

Ovulation: Swelling at the last third of the body that lasts for about 12 to 24 hours. A pre-lay shed will follow approximately 15 days later.

Egg Laying: Approximately 28 days after the pre-lay shed.

Clutch Size: 1-11 eggs

Incubation: Approximately 60 days

Recommended Incubation Temperatures: 80 to 84 degrees Fahrenheit

Recommended Incubation Humidity Levels: 90 to 100 percent

Length at Birth: 20 to 30 cm

Weight at Birth: 65 to 103 grams

Index

D

E

F

G

H

I

R

S

T

Photo Credits

Page 1 Photo by sipa via Pixabay.com
<https://pixabay.com/en/snake-ball-python-python-regius-419043/>

Page 11 Photo by Kapa65 via Pixabay.com
<https://pixabay.com/en/snake-ball-python-garden-camouflage-365039/>

Page 18 Photo by Die_Sonja via Pixabay.com
<https://pixabay.com/en/snake-ball-python-scale-constrictor-358244/>

Page 33 Photo by martinlyon via Pixabay.com
<https://pixabay.com/en/ball-python-snake-normal-reptile-210054/>

Page 43 Photo by Kapa65 via Pixabay.com
<https://pixabay.com/en/snake-python-ball-python-animal-660781/>

Page 53 Photo by Kapa65 via Pixabay.com
<https://pixabay.com/en/snake-python-ball-python-cute-732113/>

Page 62 Photo by sipa via Pixabay.com
<https://pixabay.com/en/snake-python-python-regius-
    mojave-1644072//>

Page 68 Photo by sipa via Pixabay.com
 <https://pixabay.com/en/snake-ball-python-python-regius-
    605344/>

Page 75Photo by sipa via Pixabay.com
 <https://pixabay.com/en/snake-python-ball-python-cute-
    736403/>

Page 86 Photo by Soundfrau via Pixabay
<https://pixabay.com/en/ball-python-python-regius-snake-
    401597/>

Page 94 Photo by Kapa65 via Pixabay.com
 <https://pixabay.com/en/snake-ball-python-garden-
    camouflage-365037/>

References

"An assessment of the impact of the pet trade on five CITES-
Appendix II case studies." Tomás Waller.
<https://cites.org/sites/default/files/eng/com/ac/28/E-AC28-
14-01_Annex3.pdf>

"Ball python." Petco.
<http://www.petco.com/content/petco/PetcoStore/en_US/pet
-services/resource-center/caresheets/ball-python.html>

"Ball Python Care." Kevin McCurley.
<http://www.reptilesmagazine.com/Care-Sheets/Snakes/Ball-
Python/>

"Ball Pythons." Melissa Kaplan.
<http://www.anapsid.org/ball.html>

"Ball Python." Russ Gurley, Clarice Brough CRS
<http://animalworld.com/encyclo/reptiles/snakes/ballpython
.php>

"Ball Python (Python regius) Basic Husbandry and Feeding: Housing, Diet, Handling, and Care." Drs. Foster & Smith. <http://www.peteducation.com/article.cfm?c=17+1831&aid=2 422>

"Ball Python." Snake Facts. <http://snake-facts.weebly.com/ball-python.html>

"Ball Pythons Ovulation." LivingArtReptiles <http://livingartreptiles.tripod.com/id97.html>

"Ball python Python regius." Christian A. S. Toudonou. <https://cites.unia.es/cites/file.php/1/files/id_material/assess ment_impact_pet_trade_case_study_Python_regius.pdf>

"Ball Python Morph History." DAVE AND TRACY BARKER. <http://www.reptilesmagazine.com/Ball-Python-Morph-History/>

"Ball Pythons." Lianne McLeod, DVM <http://exoticpets.about.com/cs/pythons/a/ballpythons.htm>

"Ball pythons." Banfield Pet Hospital.
<https://www.banfield.com/Banfield/media/PDF/Downloads
/Ball-Pythons.pdf>

"Ball Python Care." Ball Python Cafe.
<http://www.ballpythoncafe.com/ball-python-care.html>

"Care Sheet." Joel Bortz.
<http://www.worldofballpythons.com/python-regius/care-
sheet/>

"Choosing a Pet Snake." Lianne McLeod, DVM.
<http://exoticpets.about.com/cs/snakes/a/snakesaspets.htm>

"Detailed Discussion of Trade in Wild-Caught Reptiles."
James Green.
<https://www.animallaw.info/article/detailed-discussion-
international-trade-wild-caught-reptiles>

"Exotic Pets." Lauren Slater
<http://ngm.nationalgeographic.com/2014/04/exotic-
pets/slater-text>

"FAQ's." Allchondros.com
<http://www.allchondros.com/faq.htm>

"Feeding Your Snake." PetSmart
<http://pets.petsmart.com/guides/snakes/feeding.shtml>

"Feeding ball pythons." World of Ball Pythons.
<http://www.worldofballpythons.com/articles/feeding-ball-pythons/>

"Finding a reputable snake breeder online." PetSnakes.com
<http://pet-snakes.com/finding-reputable-snake-breeder-online>

"Glossary." The Reptilian.co.uk.
<http://www.thereptilian.co.uk/the_reptilian_glossary.html>

"Glossary of Herpetological Terms." RatSnake Foundation.
<http://www.ratsnakefoundation.org/index.php/glossary-of-herpetological-terms>

"Habitats: Cleaning and Disinfecting Reptile Cages."
PetEducation.com.
<http://www.peteducation.com/article.cfm?c=17+1796&aid=2847>

"How Do Snakes Maintain Homeostasis?" Pets on Mom.Me.
<http://animals.mom.me/snakes-maintain-homeostasis-8859.html>

"How to Bathe a Snake." Cuteness Pets Editor.
   <https://www.cuteness.com/article/bathe-snake>

"How to Bathe a Snake." PetSnakes.com.

<http://pet-snakes.com/bathe-snake>

"How to Choose Your First Pet Snake." PetHelpful.
   <https://pethelpful.com/reptiles-amphibians/Choosing-
   Your-First-Pet-Snake>

"How to Clean a Snake Cage Quickly and Easily." Reptile
   Knowledge.
   <http://www.reptileknowledge.com/news/how-to-clean-a-
   snake-cage-quickly-and-easily/>

"Husbandry for Boas & Pythons." Avian and Exotic Animal
   Care.

<http://www.avianandexotic.com/care-
   sheets/reptiles/husbandry-for-boas-pythons/>

"Looking for a Pet Reptile? Consider a Breeder." Erik J.
   Martin.
   <http://www.reptilesmagazine.com/Looking-for-a-Pet-
   Reptile-Consider-a-Breeder/>

"Reptile Tank Heating and Lighting Guide." Instructables.
<http://www.instructables.com/id/Reptile-tank-heating-and-lighting-guide/?ALLSTEPS>

"Snake Care Guide." LoveThatPet.
<https://www.lovethatpet.com/small-pets/snakes/>

"Snake Habitats, How to Create." Doctors Foster and Smith.
<http://www.drsfostersmith.com/PIC/Article.cfm?d=157&category=630&articleid=2383>

"So you think you want a pet snake?" robinsfyi.com.
<http://www.robinsfyi.com/animals/herps/soyouwantasnake.htm>

"Summary of State Laws Relating to Private Possession of Exotic Animals." Born Free USA.
<http://www.bornfreeusa.org/b4a2_exotic_animals_summary.php>

"The real cost of keeping a snake." PetSnakes.com.
<http://pet-snakes.com/cost-of-keeping-a-snake>

"The Modern U.S. Reptile Industry." Ariel H. Collis, M.A. & Robert N. Fenili
<http://m.kelleydrye.com/email/TheModernUSReptileIndustry_GES_Collis_05122011.pdf>

"The Natural History of the Ball Python, Python regius: Ball Pythons in the Wild." Frank Indiviglio.
<http://blogs.thatpetplace.com/thatreptileblog/2009/01/07/the-natural-history-of-the-ball-python-python-regius-ball-pythons-in-the-wild-part-1/#.WFAiR7J97IU>

"The real cost of keeping a snake." Pet Snakes.
<http://pet-snakes.com/cost-of-keeping-a-snake>

"What it Costs to Own a Reptile." Pet Place.
<http://www.petplace.com/article/reptiles/general/adopting-or-purchasing-a-reptile/what-it-costs-to-own-a-reptile>

"Which Exotic Pets Are Legal in the United States?" Melissa A. Smith.
<https://pethelpful.com/exotic-pets/Where-are-Exotic-Pets-Legal>

Feeding Baby
Cynthia Cherry
978-1941070000

Axolotl
Lolly Brown
978-0989658430

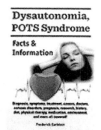

Dysautonomia, POTS
Syndrome
Frederick Earlstein
978-0989658485

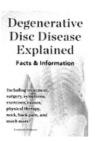

Degenerative Disc
Disease Explained
Frederick Earlstein
978-0989658485

Sinusitis, Hay Fever,
Allergic Rhinitis Explained
Frederick Earlstein
978-1941070024

Wicca
Riley Star
978-1941070130

Zombie Apocalypse
Rex Cutty
978-1941070154

Capybara
Lolly Brown
978-1941070062

Eels As Pets
Lolly Brown
978-1941070167

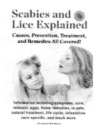

Scabies and Lice Explained
Frederick Earlstein
978-1941070017

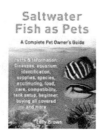

Saltwater Fish As Pets
Lolly Brown
978-0989658461

Torticollis Explained
Frederick Earlstein
978-1941070055

Kennel Cough
Lolly Brown
978-0989658409

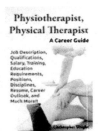

Physiotherapist, Physical
Therapist
Christopher Wright
978-0989658492

Rats, Mice, and Dormice
As Pets
Lolly Brown
978-1941070079

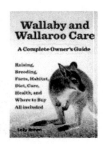

Wallaby and Wallaroo Care
Lolly Brown
978-1941070031

Bodybuilding Supplements
Explained
Jon Shelton
978-1941070239

Demonology
Riley Star
978-19401070314

Pigeon Racing
Lolly Brown
978-1941070307

Dwarf Hamster
Lolly Brown
978-1941070390

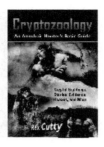

Cryptozoology
Rex Cutty
978-1941070406

Eye Strain
Frederick Earlstein
978-1941070369

Inez The Miniature Elephant
Asher Ray
978-1941070353

Vampire Apocalypse
Rex Cutty
978-1941070321

Made in the USA
Middletown, DE
21 December 2020

29446585R10076